FUNHOUSE • P!NK

ISBN 978-1-4234-6833-2

HAL•LEONARD®
CORPORATION
7777 W. BLUEMOUND RD. P.O. BOX 13819 MILWAUKEE, WI 53213

In Australia Contact:
Hal Leonard Australia Pty. Ltd.
4 Lentara Court
Cheltenham, Victoria, 3192 Australia
Email: ausadmin@halleonard.com.au

Visit Hal Leonard Online at
www.halleonard.com

SO WHAT

Words and Music by ALECIA MOORE,
MAX MARTIN and JOHAN SCHUSTER

Na, na, na, na, na, na, na,

na, na, na, na, na, na. Na, na, na, na, na, na, na, na, na, na, na, na, na. I

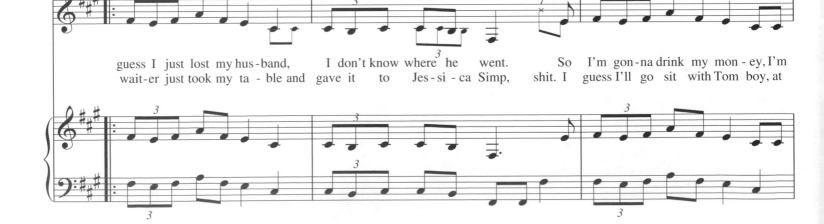

guess I just lost my hus-band, I don't know where he went. So I'm gon-na drink my mon-ey, I'm
wait-er just took my ta-ble and gave it to Jes-si-ca Simp, shit. I guess I'll go sit with Tom boy, at

not gon - na pay his rent, nope. I got a brand - new at - ti - tude and I'm gon - na wear it to - night.
least he'll know how to hit. What if this song's on the ra - di - o, then some - bod - y's gon - na die.

I'm gon - na get in trou - ble, I wan - na start a fight. Na, na, na, na, na, na, na,
I'm gon - na get in trou - ble, my ex will start __ a fight. Na, na, na, na, na, na, na,

I wan - na start a fight. Na, na, na, na, na, na, na, I wan - na start a fight. } So,
he's gon - na start a fight. Na, na, na, na, na, na, na, we're all gon - na get in a fight. } So,

A5   C#5   F#5

so what? I'm still a rock star. I got my rock moves and I don't

D.S. al Coda

SOBER

Words and Music by ALECIA MOORE,
KARA DioGUARDI, NATHANIEL HILLS
and MARCELLA ARAICA

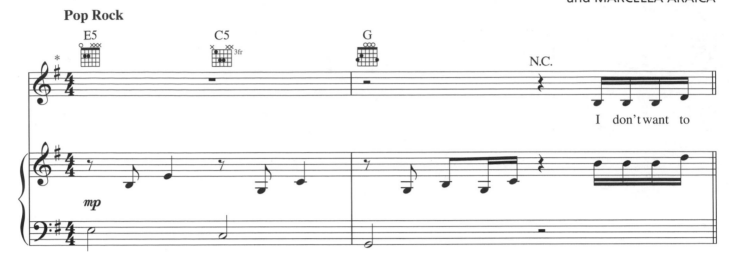

* Recorded a half step lower.

I DON'T BELIEVE YOU

Words and Music by ALECIA MOORE
and MAX MARTIN

I don't mind it, _____
I don't mind it, _____

_____ I don't mind at all. _____
I still don't mind at all. _____

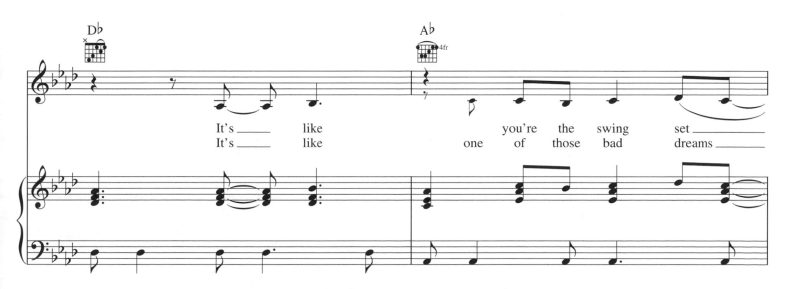

It's _____ like you're the swing set _____
It's _____ like one of those bad dreams _____

ONE FOOT WRONG

Words and Music by ALECIA MOORE
and FRANCIS EG WHITE

With a groove

Am I sweat - ing, ___ or are ___ these tears ___ on ___ my face? ___
Does an - y - one see ___ this? ___ Luck - y me, I guess I'm ___ the cho - sen one. ___

___ Should I be hun - gry? ___ I can't re-mem-ber the last ___ time that ___ I ate. ___
___ Col - or and mad - ness, ___ first in line ___ I put ___ my mon - ey down. ___

you'll have to love me when I'm gone.

You'll have to love me when I'm gone.

Vocal tacet on repeats

Repeat and Fade

Optional Ending

PLEASE DON'T LEAVE ME

Words and Music by ALECIA MOORE
and MAX MARTIN

Upbeat Pop-Rock

Da da da da, _____ da da da da. _____

Da da da _____ da da.

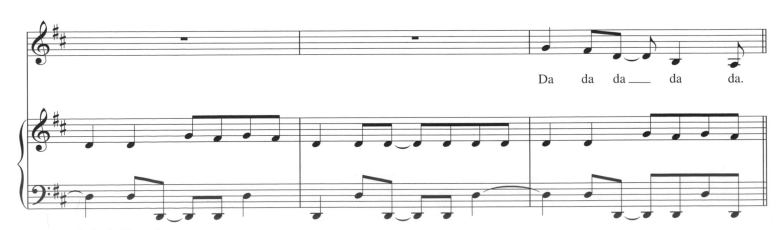

Da da da _____ da da.

Recorded a half step lower.

BAD INFLUENCE

Words and Music by ALECIA MOORE,
BUTCH WALKER, BILLY MANN
and MACHOPSYCHO

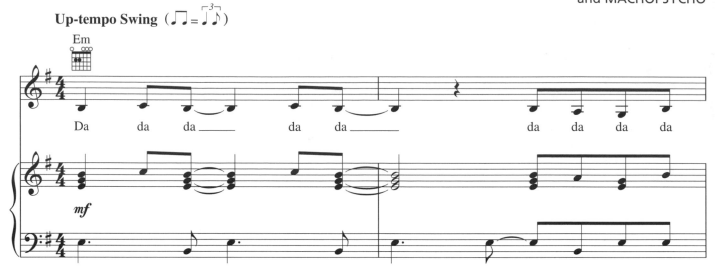

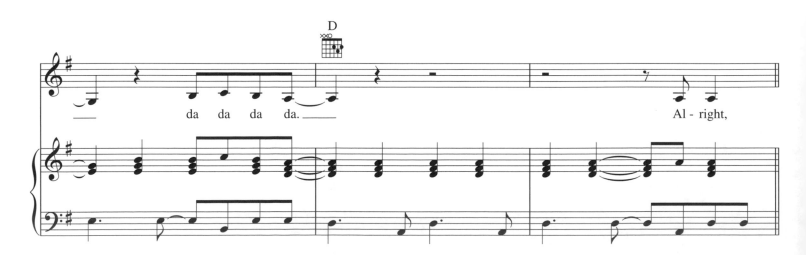

where she stops, no-bod-y knows. A good ex-cuse to be a bad in-flu-ence on

you and _____ you. _____

I'm a good ex-cuse _____ to be a bad in-flu-

-ence on you _____ and you _____ and you. _____

FUNHOUSE

Words and Music by ALECIA MOORE,
TONY KANAL and JIMMY HARRY

Funk Rock

CRYSTAL BALL

Words and Music by ALECIA MOORE
and BILLY MANN

Acoustic Folk

drink-ing wine and think-ing bliss is on the oth-er side of this,
Some-times you think ev-'ry-thing is wrapped in-side a dia-mond ring,

I'm

I just need a com-pass and a will-ing ac-com-plice.
love just needs a wit-ness and a lit-tle for-give-ness and a

cracks in the crys-tal ball. ___

I - ro - ny, ___

i - ro - ny ___ is hat - ing love, ___ hat - ing love ___ for what it

does to me, ___ what it's done to me, ___ what it's done, ___

MEAN

Words and Music by ALECIA MOORE
and BUTCH WALKER

used to hold the door for me, now you can't wait to leave. You
Al - ways sen - ti - men - tal when I think of how it was, when

IT'S ALL YOUR FAULT

Words and Music by ALECIA MOORE,
MAX MARTIN and JOHAN SCHUSTER

AVE MARY A

Words and Music by ALECIA MOORE,
BILLY MANN and PETE WALLACE

Mo-tor-cy-cles in the park-ing lot, __ rev-ving their en - gines and it just won't stop.
Bro-ken hearts __ all a-round the spot, __ I can't help __ think-ing that we lost the plot.

D.S. al Coda

go ___ of the cha - os a - round ___ me, the dev - il that hounds ___ me. I need ___

___ you to tell ___ me, ___ child, be still. ___

Child, be still. ___

CODA

A - ve Mar - y

GLITTER IN THE AIR

Words and Music by ALECIA MOORE
and BILLY MANN

Have you ev-er fed a lov-er with just your __ hands? __
Have you ev-er hat-ed your-self for star-ing at the phone?

Closed __ your eyes __ and __ trust-ed, just trust-ed?
Your whole __ life wait-ing on the ring to prove you're not a-lone?

point of no re-turn, the tip of the ice-berg, the
point of o-bliv-i-on, the ho-ur-glass on the ta-ble, the

sun be-fore the burn. The thun-der be-fore the light-ning, and the
walk be-fore the run. The breath be-fore the kiss, and the

breath be-fore the phrase. Have you ev-er felt this way?
fear be-fore the phrase. Have you ev-er felt this way?